What I Saw in
Glacier

Text by Ellen Horowitz   Photographs by Christopher Cauble

The Exploration of

_____

(Explorer, A.K.A. your name here)

/ / to / /
(Dates of exploration)

RIVERBEND
PUBLISHING

What I Saw in Glacier
© 2017 by Riverbend Publishing
Text by Ellen Horowitz
Photographs by Christopher Cauble, www.caublephotography.com
Published by Riverbend Publishing, Helena, Montana

Design by Sarah Cauble, www.sarahcauble.com

ISBN 13: 978-1-60639-099-3

Printed in the United States of America

3 4 5 6 7 8 9 0 VP 25 24 23 22

Riverbend Publishing
P.O. Box 5833
Helena, MT 59604
1-866-787-2363
www.riverbendpublishing.com

Dedication

To my parents, Marge and Joe—
It all began with the flowers on Windy Ridge.

Acknowledgments

My sincere thanks go to wildlife biologist Vicki Forristal, botanist Maria Mantis, geologist Ashley Mason and Glacier Park naturalist Bill Schustrom for their enthusiasm and willingness to review the manuscript. To Mark Wagner, Hudson Bay District Naturalist and Laura Law, GNP Education Specialist, I'm grateful for your time and expertise. A special thank you goes to the good folks at Riverbend Publishing for guidance on this project. And last, but not least, muchas gracias to Beth Judy, chief instigator.

About the Author

An outdoor educator whose career spans more than 35 years, Ellen Horowitz teaches preschoolers to adults about the wildflowers and wildlife of the Rocky Mountains. Montana Audubon has honored her with their Educator of the Year Award for her work as a natural history instructor at Flathead Valley Community College, the Glacier Institute and Road Scholar. In addition, she has received awards for her magazine writing from Outdoor Writers Association of America and the National Wildlife Federation. *What I Saw in Glacier* is her first book. Ellen lives on a farm in Columbia Falls, Montana, with her husband, their Australian cattle dog and six mules.

About the Photographer

Christopher Cauble grew up in Montana, where he began his passion for photography by exploring the mountains with a 35mm film camera passed down from his parents. After graduating from the University of Montana, he became a freelance photographer working mostly in Montana and Yellowstone National Park. His work has been featured in magazines and books, including *Yellowstone: A Land of Wild and Wonder*, *A Montana Journal*, and the popular children's book, *What I Saw In Yellowstone*. Cauble is also a nature cinematographer and his videos have been published on many national and international news sites and television programs. He lives in Livingston, Montana. His work can be found at www.caublephotography.com and on social media.

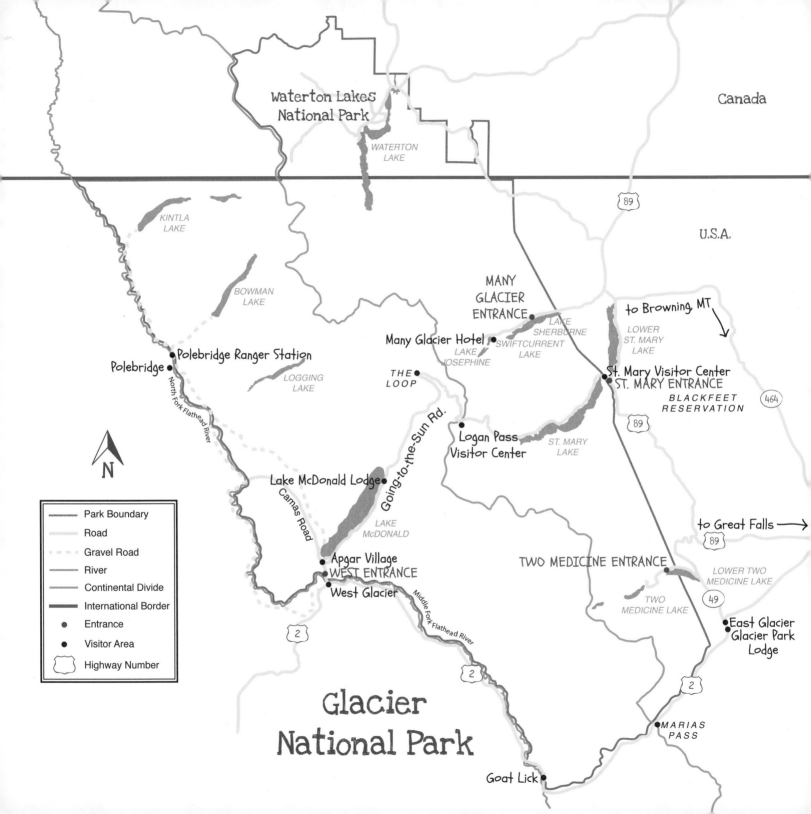

Waterton Lakes National Park

Canada

WATERTON LAKE

89

U.S.A.

KINTLA LAKE

BOWMAN LAKE

MANY GLACIER ENTRANCE

LAKE SHERBURNE

to Browning, MT

LOWER ST. MARY LAKE

Polebridge Ranger Station

Many Glacier Hotel

SWIFTCURRENT LAKE

LAKE JOSEPHINE

St. Mary Visitor Center
ST. MARY ENTRANCE

Polebridge

LOGGING LAKE

THE LOOP

464

North Fork Flathead River

BLACKFEET RESERVATION

89

Logan Pass Visitor Center

ST. MARY LAKE

to Great Falls →

89

Lake McDonald Lodge

Going-to-the-Sun Rd.

Camas Road

TWO MEDICINE ENTRANCE

LAKE McDONALD

LOWER TWO MEDICINE LAKE

Apgar Village
WEST ENTRANCE

West Glacier

TWO MEDICINE LAKE

49

Middle Fork Flathead River

East Glacier
Glacier Park Lodge

2

━━━	Park Boundary
━━━	Road
┉┉┉	Gravel Road
━━━	River
━━━	Continental Divide
━━━	International Border
●	Entrance
●	Visitor Area
⬡	Highway Number

2

N

2

MARIAS PASS

Glacier National Park

Goat Lick

Contents

Introduction

Glacier is part of Waterton-Glacier International Peace Park. Waterton Lakes National Park is a national park in Alberta, Canada, just across the border from Glacier. In 1932, the two parks became the world's first international park, a symbol of the peace and friendship between the United States and Canada. The international park also celebrates a shared ecosystem where everything in nature—plants, animals, and their environment—is connected.

Glacier National Park covers more than one million acres—an area bigger than the state of Rhode Island! The Rocky Mountains wind their way along the entire length of the park. The west and east sides of Glacier are like two different worlds. They have different weather and scenery.

The west side of the park gets more rain, so forests grow thicker and trees grow taller. You can even walk in a rainforest-like setting among 500-year-old trees.

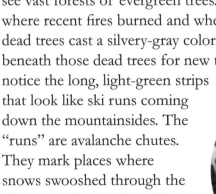
Canoers on Lake McDonald

The east side of Glacier is drier. It receives more wind and sun so the forests are more open. It's where prairies meet mountains.

Several roads take you into different parts of the park, but Going-to-the-Sun Road is the only one that crosses the entire park. As you travel this road up into the mountains, you'll notice that temperatures become cooler. The winter season in the high mountains lasts for more than half the year. Flowers here bloom later than those growing at lower elevations.

Along the drive, you'll see vast forests of evergreen trees. Watch for places where recent fires burned and where the trunks of dead trees cast a silvery-gray color on the slopes. Look beneath those dead trees for new trees and plants. And notice the long, light-green strips that look like ski runs coming down the mountainsides. The "runs" are avalanche chutes. They mark places where snows swooshed through the dark green forests, knocking down big trees in their paths.

While you're here, don't forget to look at the night sky. Glacier National Park is a famous

Beargrass

Mountain Goat Kid

place for stargazing. Look for the Milky Way, constellations, or meteors streaking across the darkness.

What I Saw in Glacier can't possibly cover everything you'll see—that would take many, many volumes. But use this book as a guide while you explore the park by car, free shuttle bus, and foot. See how many items you can check off.

Welcome to Glacier!

★ Tips for spotting wildlife: Look for movement. Many animals blend in with their environment, making them hard to see.

★ If you notice movement, look again. You might have spotted an animal turning its head, flicking an ear, or dashing by.

★ And look for colors and shapes that seem out of place. A small white speck on a mountain might be a mountain goat.

Red bus on the Going-to-the-Sun Road

Running Eagle Falls

Mountain Goat

Where to see them

Look for goats near **Logan Pass**, the **Hidden Lake Trail**, and **Goat Lick Bridge** along Highway 2.

(Oreamnos americanus)

Mountain goats are the superstars of Glacier. They live in the high country among snowy peaks and rocky cliffs. These steep places are too dangerous for most predators, but mountain goats walk along cliffs with ease. Special adaptations help mountain goats survive in this rugged, wintry world.

The goat's feet are designed for travel over rocks and snow. Its split hooves are 2 toes that spread wide. The outside of the hoof is hard, and the bottom of each toe has a soft, flexible traction pad for gripping. Two stubby dewclaws on the back of each leg act like emergency brakes when the goat is descending steep, slick slopes.

The mountain goat's white coat is made up of two kinds of fur. The outer fur is more than four-inches long and acts like a parka. A dense wooly undercoat is like long underwear. The fur protects the goat from icy winds, blowing snow, and below-zero temperatures that are part of alpine (high mountain) weather.

In summer, these four-footed mountaineers shed their thick winter fur. Shedding makes the goats look scruffy for a while. Billies (males) shed earlier than nannies (females). If you see a goat with a shaggy coat of clumped fur in July or early August, it's probably a nanny with her kid (baby goat). While hiking, look for bits of white, wooly goat fur snagged on trees and shrubs.

Both male and female mountain goats have thin, pointed black horns. The goats look similar, except billies are larger and have longer beards than nannies. Billies are often solitary or part of a small group of males. Nannies, kids, and yearling goats often travel together in bands. Kids are born in late May or early June. Within hours of birth they can jump and hop. Their very first climb might take them up the sloping, snow-colored backs of their sleeping moms! Play helps them practice skills they need for survival.

Mountain goats are herbivores (plant eaters). Their diet includes grasses, woody plants, flowers, mosses, and lichens. They also lick salt and minerals found in soil. During winter they find places where the wind blows away the snow so it's easier to find food.

Guess What?

The Great Northern Railway, which transported the first visitors to Glacier more than 100 years ago, used the mountain goat as its symbol.

Mountain goat kid

8

☐ I saw mountain goats!

Where?

When?

How many?

What were they doing?

Bighorn Sheep

(Ovis canadensis)

Where to see them

Look in meadows and steep rocky slopes around **Logan Pass**, **Many Glacier Hotel**, and **Two Medicine Valley**.

Bighorn sheep are named for the large, heavy horns of the rams (males). These horns can weigh more than 30 pounds. The horns of ewes (females) are smaller, narrower, and less curved. Bighorn sheep are also recognized by their stocky body covered with short, thick, brown to gray-brown fur. A white rump patch covers their hind ends.

Bighorn sheep live in the mountains on the east side of Glacier. They feed on plants in grassy meadows located near rocky terrain. Like mountain goats, bighorn sheep are good climbers. Bounding up steep, boulder-covered slopes helps them escape predators such as coyotes, wolves, and mountain lions. When winter approaches, bighorns mi-

Ewe

grate to lower slopes to find food. They seek places where wind whisks away the snow and exposes the plants.

Rams spend most of the year in bachelor groups. The ewes, their lambs (babies), and immature animals stay together in nursery groups. Young rams join the older rams at about age three. Young females stay with their mother's herd.

Sheep are experts at hiding in plain sight. They can be hard to see because their fur matches the color of the rocks where they like to hang out. When scanning for them, look for movement, a white rump, or the ram's curled horns.

Guess What?

In the autumn mating ritual of bighorn sheep, rams run toward each other at full speed and slam heads together. Fortunately, their thick skulls protect their brains. The sound of crashing horns can be heard from a mile away!

Ram

☐ I saw bighorn sheep!

Where?

When?

How many?

What were they doing?

11

White-Tailed Deer

(Odocoileus virginianus)

Where to see them

White-tailed deer are found all around the park. Look for mule deer in the mountains along **Going-to-the-Sun Road** and in the **St. Mary**, **Many Glacier**, and **Two Medicine** valleys.

Mule Deer

(Odocoileus hemionus)

Two species of deer live in Glacier National Park: white-tailed deer and mule deer. White-tailed deer are

Mule deer have large mule-like ears. They also have a white rump patch and a narrow black-tipped tail.

The bucks' (males) antlers are different, too. White-tailed antlers have a main beam with points sticking up from them. Mule deer antlers are forked.

There's another way to identify a deer if you don't get a look at head or tail

more common. They're found throughout the park's lower elevation forests, meadows, and river bottoms. Mule deer, or "muleys" as they're sometimes called, prefer higher elevations and more open country.

Telling the difference between white-tailed and mule deer is a matter of heads and tails. White-tailed deer have shorter ears and a larger tail. When startled, this deer runs with its tail sticking straight up. The white underside looks like a waving white flag.

as it runs by. When a mule deer is in a hurry, it bounds on all four feet at the same time. It looks like it has pogo sticks for legs: *boing, boing, boing*. This strange gait is called "stotting."

Guess What?

There's a difference between antlers and horns. Antlers are shed each year, but horns stay on and grow throughout an animal's life. Deer, elk, and moose have antlers. Mountain goats and bighorn sheep have horns.

☐ I saw deer!

What kind?

Where?

How many?

What were they doing?

Where to see them

Swiftcurrent, **Josephine**, and Fishercap lakes in **Many Glacier Valley** are good places to check. Also look in the **Two Medicine Valley** near the beaver ponds on the way toward **Aster Park**.

Moose

(Alces alces)

The moose is the largest member of the deer family, weighing up to 1,000 pounds. Besides its great size, a moose can be recognized by its dark, burly body, and long legs. Powerful shoulder muscles give it a hump-backed appearance. A bull (male) moose also carries a pair of broad, flat antlers. Like its smaller cousins, deer and elk, only the male has antlers.

Moose are at home on land and in water. Their long legs and large feet are ideal for travel through deep snow, marshy ground, or swimming across a lake. They can easily jump over fallen trees.

During summer, moose spend lots of time around lakes and ponds where they feed on nutritious water plants. They also use the water to escape from pesky mosquitos and biting flies, or to cool off on a hot afternoon. Moose can stay underwater for more than 30 seconds and dive to 18 feet deep!

Bull moose

For most of the year, moose eat all kinds of woody plants including willow, aspen, and cottonwood. "Moose" is an Algonquin Indian word meaning "twig eater."

Moose are usually seen alone or in small groups. A cow (female) moose is extremely protective of her calf (baby). Keep your distance from all moose.

☐ I saw a moose!

Where?

When?

What was it doing?

Guess what?

A moose can run at speeds up to 35 miles per hour and swim 6 miles per hour.

Black Bear

(Ursus americanus)

Where to see them

Look into the forests along **Camas Road**, **Going-to-the-Sun Road**, and **Many Glacier Road**. In late summer and fall look on mountain slopes in the **Many Glacier Valley**.

Not all black bears are black. In Glacier, their fur can be blond, light brown, cinnamon, dark brown, or jet black.

Black bears are rarely found near grizzlies, but both kinds of bears share the park. One of the best ways to tell the difference between them is to look at their rumps and shoulder humps. A black bear's rump is slightly higher than its shoulders. A grizzly bear's shoulder hump is higher than its rump.

Black bears are expert tree climbers. Short curved claws help them grip tree trunks. Trees are good places for them to snooze or hide from predators (including grizzlies). But that's not all. Black bears climb aspen and cottonwood trees in springtime to feast on the trees' tender young buds. Look for their claw marks on tree trunks.

When it comes to food, black bears are omnivores. That means they eat both plants and animals. Black bears in Glacier mainly dine on plants. In early spring they chow down on grass, dandelions, and the inner bark of pine trees. During summer, they gobble up all kinds of berries. Black bears eat rodents, other animals, and carrion (a dead animal) when available. Ants and hornets are also on the menu.

Bears consume lots of food to fatten up before going into winter dens. Their survival depends on it. For dens, they use hollow trees, fallen logs, and caves, or they dig their own dens in the ground, often among the roots of large trees.

Guess What?

In her den during January or February, a mother black bear gives birth to cubs. She might have one, two, or three cubs. Each cub weighs less than one pound when born.

☐ I saw a black bear!

Where?

When?

What was it doing?

Where to see them

Look for grizzlies in the meadows and open slopes along the **Many Glacier Road** and the **Going-to-the-Sun Road**.

Grizzly Bear

(Ursus arctos)

Mountain men called the grizzly "silvertip" because the tips of the bear's hairs are lighter in color than the rest of the hair. The two-toned hair gives a "grizzled" (grayish) look which is another explanation for the bear's name. Grizzly bear fur ranges in color from blond to black, but it's usually medium brown (with silver tips). A grizzly's distinctive shoulder hump is made up of big, powerful muscles used for digging.

Grizzly claws are up to 4 inches long. That's longer than your fingers! Long claws are useful for digging

a winter den and for digging up yummy things to eat. The long claws work like garden tools to unearth the roots of plants. (Most of a grizzly's diet comes from plants.) Those lengthy nails are also perfect for scooping out hibernating ground squirrels tucked away in burrows. A grizzly, like its smaller cousin the black bear, is an omnivore.

In late summer, some grizzlies climb mountain peaks to feed on swarms of army cutworm moths. The moths, plump from sipping nectar from wildflowers, are an excellent source of protein and fat. A single bear can snarf up as many as 40,000 moths in a day!

☐ I saw a grizzly bear!

Where?

When?

What was it doing?

Guess What?

A mother bear teaches her cubs what to eat and where to find food. Grizzly cubs stay with their mother until they're about 2½ years old. Male bears do not help raise their cubs.

Beaver

(Castor canadensis)

Where to see them

Look for beavers along **Lower McDonald Creek**, **St. Mary River** footbridge (located between the campground and visitor center), and **Swiftcurrent Lake** in the **Many Glacier Valley**.

In Glacier, you can find lots of evidence of beaver activity. But your best chance of seeing a beaver is evening or early morning. That's because beavers work at night and sleep during the day.

Beavers live along lakes, ponds, and streams. They cut trees for food, shelter, and building dams. Chewing wood also keeps their ever-growing teeth from getting too long.

The beaver's chisel-sharp teeth chomp through tree trunks, leaving large splinters of wood on the ground. Trees cut down by beavers appear as pointed stumps complete with tooth marks. In some places, you can find stumps that are 3- to 4-feet tall. A tall stump is a clue that the tree was cut in winter. The beaver simply walked on top of the snow.

Beavers build their lodges from sticks and mud. Lodges are places to sleep, give birth to kits (babies), hide from predators, and stay warm in winter. They enter and exit the lodge from underwater.

A beaver dam is also built from sticks and mud, but it's different than a lodge. The dam is built to hold back water in a stream to form a pond. A deep pond provides a safe place for beavers to escape from most predators. Coyotes, mountain lions, black bears, grizzly bears, and wolves prey on beavers.

Photo courtesy National Park Service

Guess What?

A beaver pond is a great place to look for moose. That's because moose like to eat willows that grow around the edges of ponds.

☐ I saw a beaver!

Where?

When?

What was it doing?

16

Golden-mantled Ground Squirrel

(Callospermophilus lateralis)

Where to see them

Columbian ground squirrels are found throughout the park. Look for golden-mantled ground squirrels at **Hidden Lake Overlook** and **Sun Point**.

One ground squirrel found in Glacier is the golden-mantled ground squirrel. Because of its black and white stripes, people often mistake this squirrel for a super-sized chipmunk. But look carefully. Notice how its white stripes start at the shoulders. A chipmunk's stripes start by its eyes.

The golden-mantled ground squirrel lives in the mountains. It usually digs its burrow beneath rocks, stumps, and logs. Except for a mother squirrel with young, golden-mantled ground squirrels spend most of their time alone.

Golden-mantled ground squirrel

☐ I saw a ground squirrel!

What kind?

Where?

When?

What was it doing?

Columbian Ground Squirrel

(Urocitellus columbianus)

Columbian ground squirrels are the most commonly seen mammals in Glacier during summer. Meadows and sunny edges of forests are places to find them. Ground squirrels don't climb trees, although they occasionally climb on rocks and logs to look around.

Ground squirrels live in colonies with members of their extended families. They rarely stray far from their burrows. Standing by an entrance is a safe place to watch for predators. Badgers, weasels, coyotes, foxes, hawks, and eagles are just a few of the carnivores (meat-eaters) that like to eat them. When a squirrel spots an intruder, it begins chirping an alarm call. This warning tells other squirrels to "run for cover."

Ground squirrels sleep for up to nine months of the year. That means they have only a few months to fatten up. By pigging out on plants—flowers, leaves, roots, and seeds—they gain enough weight to make it through the long winter season.

Columbian ground squirrel

Guess What?

Besides providing places to hide from predators, burrows also provide cozy quarters for ground squirrels to nap, raise their pups (babies), and hibernate.

Red Squirrel

(Tamiasciurus hudsonicus)

Where to see them

You can see (and hear) red squirrels in forests throughout the park. **Trail of the Cedars**, **Avalanche Lake Trail**, and **Swiftcurrent Nature Trail** are a few places to look. Chipmunks are seen in picnic areas and campgrounds, and along forest trails.

If you see a small, dark-colored squirrel scampering along the forest floor or scurrying up a tree, you just met the red squirrel. This brown to reddish-black animal, with a creamy-white belly and white eye rings, is often heard before it's seen. When disturbed by an intruder—other squirrels, other animals, or you—the red squirrel complains with its chattering call.

Red squirrels stay active year-round. In late summer and autumn they begin caching (storing) lots of pine cones for winter food. The huge piles, called middens, are usually heaped against a tree, log, or stump. Of course, the squirrels don't eat all the seeds in the cones. Some dropped seeds sprout and grow into trees.

As part of the forest food web, red squirrels are eaten by hawks, owls, eagles, weasels, pine martens, and lynx.

Red Squirrel

Guess What?

The chipmunk's light and dark stripes are a form of camouflage called "protective coloration." The stripes make it more difficult for predators to see the chipmunk's body shape.

Chipmunk

(Tamias species)

Chipmunks are the smallest members of the squirrel family. They're easy to recognize by size and the bold stripes on their faces and backs.

These lively little animals hardly ever sit still unless they pause to eat. They usually find food in underbrush where they're hidden from predators. Chipmunks eat seeds, plants, and berries, and they chow down on insects and some bird eggs. When feeding, chipmunks pack food into cheek pouches to store away for later meals. Cheek pouches are like built-in grocery sacks. They're handy for carrying food back to their dens.

Chipmunks hibernate in winter, but not like ground squirrels. Chipmunks wake up from time to time to nibble some of their stored food. Then they go back to sleep.

Chipmunk

☐ **I saw a red squirrel!**
☐ **I saw a chipmunk!**

Where?

When?

What was it doing?

Where to see them

Look for hoary marmots along the **Hidden Lake Trail** at **Logan Pass** during July and August, and along the **Going-to-the-Sun Road**.

(Marmota caligata)

The hoary marmot is the alpine cousin to the woodchuck. It lives near rocky slopes and mountain meadows. It's Glacier's largest member of the squirrel family, weighing up to 11 pounds.

You can recognize this high-country critter by its two-toned fur. The hoary marmot's front half is silvery-white. (The word "hoary" means "silver-gray.") The color of its back half, including its long tail, is golden-brown. The marmot's scientific name also describes something about its appearance. The word "caligata" means "booted." Although it doesn't wear boots, it has conspicuous black feet.

The hoary marmot spends most of its day either eating or sunning itself. When stretched out sunbathing on a flat rock, a marmot is hard to see. Its camouflage colors and motionless pose help keep it hidden from predators—eagles, bears, wolverines, wolves, mountain lions, and coyotes.

When feeding and moving around, a marmot is much easier to spot. Grasses, sedges (grass-like plants), and an assortment of wildflowers help it pack on the pounds. Like its smaller cousins the ground squirrels, this alpine animal must fatten up before its long winter hibernation. The hoary marmot stays snug in its burrow buried beneath deep, deep snow.

☐ I saw a hoary marmot!

Where?

When?

What was it doing?

Guess What?

Another name for the marmot is "whistler" or "whistle pig" because it gives a loud, high-pitched whistle to warn other marmots of approaching danger. The sound carries for long distances.

Gray Jay

(Perisoreus canadensis)

Gray jays are common, fascinating birds to watch in the spruce forests of Glacier. These birds travel in family groups. If you see one, keep looking, because there are probably two others nearby.

During summer, gray jays gather food and store it for winter. They eat seeds, berries, fungi, insects, and small animals. They also scavenge on dead animals. Using sticky saliva from their mouths as a "glue," gray jays cache thousands of food items under tree bark. Thanks to their great memories, jays remember where they stashed their caches. They eat from these "pantries" when other food is scarce in winter.

Gray jays are also known as camp robbers, Canada jays, and whiskey jacks. They're called camp robbers because they like to steal food from campsites. The name whisky jack comes from an Indian name, *wiss-katjon*. White settlers pronounced it "Whiskey John," then changed it to "Whiskey Jack."

Guess what?

Gray jays often carry food with their feet, which is not typical for songbirds. Songbirds usually carry food in their beaks.

Steller's Jay

(Cyanocitta stelleri)

The Steller's jay is the western cousin to the blue jay. The black crest on its head and its deep blue body and wings make it easy to recognize. Like other jays, it's bold and noisy.

Steller's jays can imitate the sounds of hawks, eagles, squirrels, dogs, and cats. They can even mimic the sound of a water sprinkler! In Glacier, if you hear the scream of a hawk when you're in the woods, look around. There's a good chance you're hearing a Steller's jay imitating a hawk. The call is used to scare away and keep other jays from entering its territory.

Photo courtesy National Park Service

☐ I saw a gray jay!
☐ I saw a Stellar's jay!

Where?

When?

What was it doing?

20

Where to see them

Ravens are found almost anywhere in the park, but often viewed near campgrounds, picnic areas, parking lots, and other places with open skies.

Common Raven

(Corvus corax)

Common ravens are the crow's big cousins. Besides size, ravens can be identified from crows by shaggy-looking feathers on their throats. Their beaks are also bigger and thicker. Another feature to look for is the shape of their tails while they fly. Ravens have diamond-shaped tails. The tails of crows are straight across at the end.

Ravens fly with strong steady wing beats. Sometimes they just soar across the sky. At other times they're acrobats that tumble and swoop through the air. Occasionally these birds fly upside-down for a few seconds!

Ravens aren't picky eaters. Seeds, berries, insects, mice, frogs, eggs, and young birds are all on their menu. They love to eat carrion and are often the first scavengers to locate it. When ravens find a large dead animal with a hide too thick for them to tear apart, they give a special call. To a predator, the call says, "Come and get it!" Wolves, grizzlies, coyotes, and other scavengers watch and listen for ravens. After one of these large animals rips into a carcass, ravens fly in and grab chunks of meat. By working together, they all share the prize.

☐ I saw a common raven!

Where?

When?

What was it doing?

Guess what?

Ravens are the largest member of the crow family, which also includes jays, magpies, and nutcrackers. Members of the crow family are considered very intelligent birds.

Bald Eagle

(Haliaeetus leucocephalus)

Where to see them

Look for bald eagles around **Lake McDonald**, **St. Mary Lake**, and along the **Middle Fork Flathead River**.

Eagles are large, powerful birds. They have been important to Native Americans' spiritual beliefs for thousands of years. Bald eagles have been the emblem of the United States since 1782.

Bald eagles stand 3 feet tall and their wingspan reaches 6 to 7 feet wide. The adult is easy to identify by its white head (covered with white feathers, not "bald"), white tail, brown body, and brown wings. Immature eagles have dark head and tail feathers. It takes about 5 years before they get their adult feather colors.

Guess What?

Other raptors in Glacier include golden eagles, hawks, falcons, ospreys, and owls.

Bald eagles mate for life. The pair builds an enormous stick nest they use year after year. Each spring they make repairs and add new sticks to it. The nest is usually built near water on top of a tall tree or on a cliff.

Eagles are classified as "raptors" and "birds of prey." That means they're birds that eat meat. All raptors have sharp, curved beaks used for tearing apart meat. They also have strong legs and toes with sharp talons to catch, crush, hold, and carry prey.

Fish are part of a bald eagle's diet. When looking for a fishy meal, the eagle swoops down and grabs one near the water's surface. Additional items on a bald eagle's menu include ducks, ground squirrels, and other small animals. Eagles also scavenge on carrion.

☐ I saw a bald eagle!

Where?

When?

What was it doing?

Huckleberry

(Vaccinium species)

Huckleberry is one of the most popular plants in Glacier because the berries are so tasty. The berries are a favorite food for grizzly and black bears. Grouse, pine martens, coyotes, foxes, chipmunks, and squirrels also like to eat them. People love huckleberries, too. They're eaten fresh, and they're used in ice cream, pies, jam, and other foods. Remember, never eat anything you can't positively identify! Be sure to check park rules about berry picking.

There are several different kinds of huckleberry bushes. The smallest ones grow about ankle tall and have tiny red berries. The largest bushes stand more than waist high. Their dark purple berries may be one-half inch in size.

Most huckleberries don't grow in clusters like their cousin the blueberry. Instead, they grow as single berries scattered along the stems of a bush. Bears spend a lot of time moving from plant to plant in a huckleberry

patch to get enough to eat. When the berries are abundant, bears get fat from feasting on them.

Hucks (as they're also known) grow best in open forests in the mountains, including places where fires burned. The first huckleberries begin to ripen on sunny slopes at low elevations in early July. They ripen at higher elevations later in the season.

☐ I saw huckleberries!

Where?

When?

How many?

What were they like?

Guess What?
The Kootenai and Blackfeet collected huckleberries in late summer. After gathering baskets or containers of berries, women and girls dried them in the sun for winter use.

23

Lodgepole Pine

(Pinus contorta)

Where to see them

Lodgepole pines grow in forests from low elevations to about midway up the mountains. Look for young lodgepole pines in recently burned forests along **Going-to-the-Sun Road** and **Camas Road**.

Lodgepole pine is one of the first evergreen trees to grow after a forest fire. That's because their seeds sprout best on bare ground where they get lots of sun.

Lodgepole has two kinds of woody cones. One type opens when it is mature, dropping its seeds to the ground. The other type of cone has a waxy coating that locks the seeds inside. This kind, called a serotinous cone, needs a fire to melt the coating. Then these cones open and their seeds fall out. New lodgepole pines begin to grow by the following spring.

This tree is important for animals. In late summer, red squirrels start gathering loads of pine cones and caching them to eat during winter. Snowshoe hares nibble the tender bark from young lodgepole during the snowy season. In springtime, some bears strip the outer bark from the trees and eat the thin, sweet inner bark called cambium (CAM-be-um).

The Blackfeet and Kootenai used lodgepole pines to make the frames for their tipis (lodges). That's how the tree got its name.

Guess What?

Lodgepole is the only pine tree in Glacier with needles that grow in bunches of two. If you move the two needles apart they form the letter "L" for lodgepole. Or, if you hold the needles like the letter "V" and turn it upside-down, they look like a tipi (or lodge).

☐ **I saw lodgepole pines!**

Where?

When?

How many?

What were they like?

Where to see them

Aspen groves thrive in the foothills and mountains on the east side of the park near **St. Mary**, **Many Glacier**, and **Two Medicine**.

Quaking Aspen

(Populus tremuloides)

Aspens are best known for the golden colors their leaves turn each autumn. But aspens are awesome for other reasons.

Recognizing them is easy. Aspens have smooth, powdery white bark. Look at a leaf and notice how it's nearly round with a point at the tip. Next, gently feel the leaf stem. It's flat, not round like most leaf stems. When the wind blows, the flattened stem flops back and forth, causing the leaf to tremble or "quake."

One amazing thing about aspens is that they're musical trees. Listen to the sounds of leaves fluttering in a breeze. Then place your

ear next to the tree's smooth trunk while the leaves shake. You'll hear a different sound. What does it remind you of?

Another surprising thing about aspen trees is that they provide food for many animals. Black bears and ruffed grouse nip aspen buds. Elk and porcupines gnaw the bark. Moose and deer chomp young trees and twigs. Beavers eat aspen bark and use the nibbled tree limbs for building dams and lodges. This leads to the next astounding thing about aspens.

When an aspen is cut down by a beaver or burned in a forest fire, part of it survives. New aspen trees sprout up from the roots of other aspens. That means each new tree in a grove is like an identical twin of the original tree.

Guess what?

Some Indian tribes called aspen by names that translated to "noisy leaf."

☐ I saw quaking aspens!

Where?

When?

How many?

What were they like?

Fireweed

Where to see them

Fireweed grows along roads, in burned areas, and in avalanche chutes.

(Chamerion angustifolium)

Fireweed is one of the first flowers to appear following a forest fire. That's how it gets its name. But fireweed also grows in other sunny places including avalanche paths and roadsides.

These showy plants stand from 3- to 6-feet tall. Up to 50 pinkish-purple flowers grow on a stem. Each flower produces hundreds of tiny seeds attached to silky fluff. Like mini parachutes, the fluff carries the seeds away. A single plant can produce 80,000 seeds! No wonder fireweed often grows in large clusters. Fireweed plants bloom from mid-summer to fall.

Guess What?

Bears, deer, elk, and chipmunks eat fireweed.

☐ I saw fireweed!

Where?

When?

How many?

What were they like?

26

Where to see them

Glacier lilies grow in forests and mountain meadows along **Going-to-the-Sun Road** and the **Many Glacier** and **Two Medicine** roads. **Logan Pass** is a great place to see them in early July.

Glacier Lily

(Erythronium grandiflorum)

Glacier lilies don't grow on glaciers, but they are one of the first flowers to appear as snow begins to melt. Glacier lilies bloom at low elevations in April. Up in the mountains, where snow lingers, they bloom in July. Huge patches of glacier lilies turn mountain meadows bright yellow with their flowers.

It's easy to recognize a glacier lily by its large yellow flower with six petals. Notice how each petal curls backwards. The glacier lily also has two long, strap-like leaves that grow at ground level.

Many animals eat glacier lilies. Grizzlies, black bears, hoary marmots, Columbian ground squirrels, deer, elk, and bighorn sheep eat the flowers, stems, and leaves. Grizzlies also love glacier lily bulbs (a type of root). They dig up the ground to expose the bulbs, and then bite them off. Of course, the bears don't eat all the bulbs. There are plenty left over.

Scientists discovered that grizzly bears actually help glacier lilies grow better. That's because grizzlies loosen the soil by digging with their long claws. Any plants or leaves that get shredded by claws are mixed back into the soil. It's like a gardener adding compost. These things—turning the soil and adding nutrients—help the remaining glacier lilies produce more seeds.

☐ I saw glacier lilies!

Where?

When?

How many?

What were they like?

Guess what?

The glacier lily is also known as avalanche lily, fawn lily, and dogtooth violet.

27

Beargrass

(Xerophyllum tenax)

Where to see them

Beargrass is found throughout the park. Watch for it along **Going-to-the-Sun Road** and the **Many Glacier** and **Two Medicine** roads.

If the park had an official flower, it would be beargrass. This impressive, sturdy plant grows up to four feet tall.

Beargrass is a wildflower full of surprises. First, beargrass isn't a grass; it's a member of the lily family. From a distance, a beargrass flower looks like one gigantic blossom. It's not. Get a close look and you'll discover the second surprise. The big blossom is actually made up of many small, creamy-white lily flowers. Up to 400 of them grow on a single plant! The dainty flowers start blooming lower on the stem and eventually open all the way to the top as the stem grows. As more flowers appear along the stem,

the overall shape of the flower cluster seems to magically change from a small ball to a tall, oblong plume.

Beargrass begins blooming in McDonald Valley in early-June. You can find it flowering in the mountains around Logan Pass in mid-July.

Some bears use beargrass leaves for bedding in their winter dens. They occasionally eat the thick white base of the leaves. Pocket gophers, ground squirrels, and mice eat the base of leaves and roots. Deer and elk like to munch the stalks and young flowers. Bees, beetles, and flower flies eat the pollen (and by doing so, they help pollinate the flowers). Chipmunks and some little birds eat the seeds.

Guess what?

Even if there are no flowers, you can identify beargrass by its large clump of dark green, grass-like leaves. These tough leaves were used by some Native Americans for basket weaving.

☐ I saw beargrass!

Where?

When?

How many?

What was it like?

Where to see them

Paintbrush is found along roadsides and forest edges, and in alpine meadows.

Indian Paintbrush

(Castilleja species)

Different kinds of Indian paintbrush grow in Glacier. Their colors can be pale yellow, orange, red, or hot pink.

Most people think the colorful part of this plant is the flower, but it's not! You'll need to look closely to find the paintbrush's very modest tube-shaped flowers. The colorful parts are a type of leaf called a bract. The bracts attract bees and butterflies.

Indian paintbrush gets its name from a Native American legend in which a young boy tries to paint the beauty of the sunset. Eventually the Great Spirit provides him with brushes filled with colors. When the boy finishes his painting, he leaves the used brushes on the land where they blossom into these colorful wildflowers.

☐ I saw Indian Paintbrush!

Where?

When?

How many?

What was it like?

Guess What?

Hoary marmots like to eat paintbrush. Bees, butterflies, and hummingbirds sip nectar from both Indian Paintbrush and Fireweed.

Going-to-the-Sun Road

Where to See it

Start at either the **St. Mary** Entrance Station on the east side of the park or by **Lake McDonald** on the west side.

Only a few miles of rutted wagon roads existed when Glacier was established in 1910. It took almost 20 years to build the entire Going-to-the-Sun Road. Work in the mountains was difficult and dangerous. Back then, machinery was primitive and moved slowly. In some places, men swung pick axes, dug with shovels, and moved rocks by hand. Stone masons dangled from ropes as they built retaining walls on the sides of cliffs. During the fall of 1932, the 50-mile road finally opened. It connected Lake McDonald Valley on the west side of the park to St. Mary Valley on the east side. It is the only road that crosses the mountains of the park. The road gets its name from Going-to-the-Sun Mountain located east of Logan Pass.

The building of the road is still considered an engineering feat. There are many amazing features to watch for. The West Side Tunnel has huge "windows" for viewing Heaven's Peak. The Loop is a tight switchback in the road. Triple Arches supports the road where it

was built out from the mountainside. And the East Side Tunnel was dug by crews using hand tools.

Each spring, Glacier park crews spend about two months clearing snow off the road. The Big Drift, located east of Logan Pass, measures up to 80 feet deep!

Guess What?

You don't have to drive the Going-to-the-Sun Road in your own car. Free shuttle busses travel the entire road and will pick you up and drop you off at many locations. Taking a bus lets you enjoy the scenery and look for wildlife.

☐ **I saw the Going-to-the-Sun Road!**

When?

What was it like?

Logan Pass

Where to see it

Take the **Going-to-the-Sun Road**. **Logan Pass** is 18 miles from **St. Mary** and 32 miles from **Lake McDonald**.

Spectacular scenery and flower-filled meadows make Logan Pass one of Glacier's most popular places to visit. Located on the Continental Divide, it is the highest point along the Going-to-the-Sun Road. At this elevation—6,646 feet above sea level—summer is short and winter lasts most of the year.

During winter, snow drifts bury the Logan Pass Visitor Center. Wind speeds can reach more than 130 miles per hour. With so much blowing snow no one knows exactly how much snow actually falls at the pass.

When Going-to-the-Sun Road opens in June, an average of six feet of snow still covers the parking lot!

Snow even blankets the meadows into early July. As it melts away, wildflowers carpet the ground with their yellow, pink, purple, and white blossoms. Flowers, grasses, and sedges provide food for many different kinds of animals, including Columbian ground squirrels. These squirrels abound near the visitor center, but take a walk and look for other critters. Mountain goats, bighorn sheep, marmots, pikas, grizzlies, and wolverines are just a few of the many animals that live here or travel through. Be sure to stay on the designated trails so you don't trample the plants.

Logan Pass was named for William Logan, Glacier National Park's first superintendent. Park rangers at the visitor center can help you identify the flowers, animals, and mountain peaks around you. Check out the interactive exhibits about high-country animals along the paved trail behind the visitor center. Trailheads for Hidden Lake and the Highline Trail begin at the pass.

Guess what?

The Canadian flag at the visitor center is a reminder that Glacier is part of Waterton–Glacier International Peace Park.

☐ I saw Logan Pass!

When?

What was it like?

Mt. Reynolds from Logan Pass

Red Buses

The red tour buses in Glacier are nicknamed "jammers." The name came from the sound of grinding metal as bus drivers shifted and "jammed" the gears on the steep, curvy Going-to-the-Sun Road.

Glacier's fleet of 33 buses was built by the White Motor Company in the 1930s. The buses were specifically designed for sightseeing in national parks. Their canvas tops rolled back so passengers could stand up to view the scenery. Each park that bought touring buses chose its own color. Glacier's buses were painted red to match the color of ripe mountain ash berries.

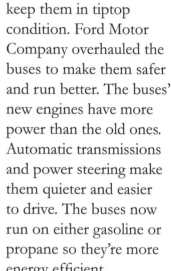

The buses still look as new as the day they arrived in the park. However, much work has been done to keep them in tiptop condition. Ford Motor Company overhauled the buses to make them safer and run better. The buses' new engines have more power than the old ones. Automatic transmissions and power steering make them quieter and easier to drive. The buses now run on either gasoline or propane so they're more energy efficient.

One thing that hasn't changed is the sight of these grand old red buses transporting visitors across Going-to-the-Sun Road. It's like stepping back in time.

Guess What?
Glacier's red buses are considered the oldest fleet of touring vehicles anywhere in the world.

☐ I saw a red bus!

Where?

When?

What was it like?

Where to see it

By road, you can cross the **Continental Divide** at **Logan Pass** on the **Going-to-the-Sun Road** and at **Marias Pass** on US Highway 2 on the park's southern boundary.

Continental Divide

The Continental Divide, sometimes called the Great Divide, runs the entire length of the North American continent from Alaska to Mexico. In Glacier National Park, it follows the rugged peaks of the Rocky Mountains. Native Americans called it "the backbone of the world."

The Continental Divide separates the flow of water in North America. Rivers west of the divide flow to the Pacific Ocean; rivers to the east flow to the Atlantic Ocean.

The Going-to-the-Sun Road crosses the Continental Divide at Logan Pass. Hikers and backpackers can

walk across the Continental Divide on several trails. One of these backcountry crossings is a mountain called Triple Divide Peak. It gets that name because water flowing from this peak goes in three directions. Some water goes west to the Pacific Ocean. Some flows northeast to Hudson's Bay in the northern Atlantic Ocean. And some water flows southeast to the Gulf of Mexico in the Atlantic Ocean. Triple Divide Peak can be seen from the Going-to-the-Sun Road. Look for the pullout near the Two Dog Flats area.

☐ I saw the Continental Divide!

When?

What was it like?

Guess what?

In Glacier, hiking trails cross the Continental Divide at Swiftcurrent Pass, Brown Pass, Gunsight Pass, Two Medicine Pass, and several other places.

Glacial Features

Where to See them

Pullouts along the **Going-to-the-Sun Road** provide great views of U-shaped valleys and horns. They can also be seen in the **Many Glacier** and **Two Medicine** valleys.

Over thousands of years, immense ice-age glaciers carved the peaks and scooped out the valleys of Glacier National Park. A glacier is a thick mass of

slow-moving ice. As it creeps along, the ice picks up rocks and gravel. This rocky rubble grinds away the land and creates distinctive landscapes—U-shaped valleys and mountain "horns."

The Lake McDonald and St. Mary valleys are good examples of U-shaped valleys

Guess What?

In some places, the ice-age glaciers that carved Glacier's landscape were so deep that only the tops of the mountains poked above them!

sculpted by huge glaciers. Many smaller glaciers left their mark by gouging out the narrower valleys found between mountains.

Another glacial feature is a horn. That's a sharp, pyramid-shaped peak formed when glaciers chisel a mountain from at least three sides. Mount Reynolds and Clements Mountain located at Logan Pass are examples of horns. Many of the most prominent mountains in Glacier are "horns."

The small glaciers found in the park continue to shape the land. One way to tell if there's nearby glacial activity is by looking at the color of a lake. Lakes with gemstone-colored water contain "rock flour." This is a fine powder of rock particles formed when a glacier grinds the bedrock beneath it. Melting glacial ice carries the rock flour into streams, and the streams take the rock flour to lakes. When sunlight reflects off the tiny rock particles, the lake water looks turquois or emerald.

"Rock flour" colors Grinnell Lake (upper left) and Upper Grinnell Lake (left) below Salamander Glacier.

A glacier-carved U-shaped valley

☐ I saw glacial features!

Where?

What type?

What were they like?

Grinnell Point, a glacial "horn"

Ancient Rocks, Ripple Marks, & Mud Cracks

Where to see them

Sedimentary rocks are everywhere in the park. Look at the cliffs along **Going-to-the-Sun Road**. **Hidden Lake Trail** at **Logan Pass** has great examples of ripple marks and mud cracks.

As crazy as it sounds, the mountains in Glacier were made from mud!

A billion and a half years ago, an inland sea covered the area that today makes up the park. Layers of fine sediments (clay, silt, and sand) settled into the water from surrounding lands during Precambrian times. (Precambrian means "before life.") Each layer was thinner than your fingernail, but over time they built up hundreds of thousands of feet thick. These sediments slowly compressed and cemented together to become "sedimentary rock." Different minerals in the rocks give them their red, green, gray, and tan colors.

Eventually, tremendous underground pressure caused the sedimentary rocks to buckle and lift upwards, creating huge mountains. During the upheaval, the oldest layers were forced over the top of younger layers and became the rocks, cliffs, and mountains in Glacier.

Scientists know these ancient rocks developed from lake mud because of evidence in the rocks. In Glacier, there are rocks that show ripple marks and mud cracks. Ripple marks are wavy patterns, formed from the back and forth movement of water over the sediments—like wave action at a beach. Mud cracks formed when the mud was exposed to air and dried out.

Mud cracks

Ripple marks on the Hidden Lake Trail

Guess What?

In Glacier you can see and touch rocks that are a billion years old!

☐ **I saw ancient rocks, ripple marks, and mud cracks!**

Where?

What were they like?

Where to see it

The pullout for Jackson Glacier is east of **Logan Pass** along **Going-to-the-Sun Road**.

In 1850, there were about 150 glaciers in the mountains that would become the park. When the park was established in 1910, it was still filled with glaciers, and that's why it was named Glacier National Park. Today there are fewer than 25 glaciers. Most of the glaciers are located far into the mountains where they can only be seen by hiking long distances. However, Jackson Glacier is visible from a pullout on the eastern side of Going-to-the-Sun Road.

Scientists are studying glaciers in the park to learn how quickly they're melting. They do this through photography. They begin by looking at historic photographs—some pictures are more than 100 years old. Then they figure out the exact place the old photo was taken. The scientists set up a camera and take pictures from that same spot. By comparing how the glaciers look in the old and new photos, scientists can measure changes in the size and shape of the glaciers.

A glacier shrinks when the amount of melting snow is more than the amount of new snow that accumulates in a year. A glacier grows when the buildup of winter snow is greater than the snow that melts in summer.

☐ I saw Jackson Glacier!

When?

What was it like?

Guess what?

Because of global warming, scientists predict that all of Glacier's remaining glaciers will be gone by 2030.

Lake McDonald

Where to see it

Lake McDonald is near the west entrance to the **Going-to-the-Sun Road**. The historic Lake McDonald Lodge is on the shoreline near the head of the lake.

Thousands of years ago, a huge glacier flowed out of the mountains. Before stopping, the glacier carved a long, winding valley with steep sides and gouged out an enormous bathtub-shaped hole. As the glacier melted, water replaced the ice. Today, this water-filled "hole" is Lake McDonald. This is the largest lake in the park—10 miles long, 1.5 miles wide, and 472 feet deep. The glacier that formed it was more than 2,000 feet thick.

The first people who spent time along the lake were Native Americans. The names they gave to lakes and other locations usually described what they were doing or what they saw. One of the Kootenai names for Lake McDonald translated to "Where people dance." They also called it "Sacred dancing water" because it was a place to hold special ceremonies. Other names included "Fish Lake" or "Lake of fishing." An interesting name given to the lake by the Blackfeet was "The bear wags its tail."

Names changed over time as mountain men, explorers, and settlers arrived in the area. The name "McDonald" came from Duncan McDonald, a fur trader who camped by the lake. In 1878 he carved his name on a tree trunk, and the carving stood out like a sign. So people began calling the lake "McDonald."

Guess What?

Lake McDonald is the lowest elevation in the park at about 3,050 feet. The distant peaks (best viewed from the foot of the lake near Apgar Village) rise up more than one mile above the lake.

☐ I saw Lake McDonald!

When?

What was it like?

Where to see them

The historic boats are found on **St. Mary Lake** (near **Rising Sun**), **Two Medicine Lake, Swiftcurrent** and **Josephine** lakes in the **Many Glacier Valley**, and **Lake McDonald**.

Historic wooden tour boats cruise the waters of several park lakes. The Glacier Park Boat Company began offering boat tours in the 1930s. From the boats, passengers view scenery (and sometimes wildlife) that just can't be seen from the road. Some of the boat rides are combined with ranger-led hikes. Check park information to find out about boat schedules and fees.

All the historic boats on the east side of Glacier are named for Blackfeet people. They are: *Morning Eagle*, *Little Chief*, *Chief Two Guns*, and *Sinopah*. On Lake McDonald, the *DeSmet* was named after a pioneering priest.

The historic boats only operate in the summer.

St. Mary Lake is a glacier-carved lake surrounded by mountains that seem to rise straight from water to sky. The Blackfeet called it by the descriptive name, "Walled-in Lakes." Melting snow from several glaciers still feed into St. Mary Lake. The turquois and emerald colors of the water come from "rock flour." (See page 36)

One of the most photographed views in the park is found along the lake. Look for the "Wild Goose Island" pullout and stop there. The view of the island, the lake, and the surrounding mountains makes a popular picture.

☐ **I saw St. Mary Lake and historic boats!**

When?

What were they like?

Guess What?

St. Mary Lake is the second largest lake in Glacier—10 miles long and 242 feet deep.

Many Glacier Hotel

Where to see it
The hotel is near the end of the road into the **Many Glacier Valley**.

The Great Northern Railway built the imposing Many Glacier Hotel more than 100 years ago. The railway advertised Glacier as the "Little Switzerland of America," and this four-story hotel on the edge of Swiftcurrent Lake was designed to look like a Swiss chalet.

In the early days of the park, visitors arrived by train and then travelled through the mountains by horseback, staying each night at a hotel or chalet. The Many Glacier Hotel was one of the largest and grandest places they stayed.

The hotel was named for the Many Glacier Valley where numerous glaciers covered the mountains. Only a few small glaciers remain today, but the glacier-carved landscape still attracts sightseers and hikers.

In addition to magnificent scenery and numerous hiking trails, visitors come to look for wildlife. From the lakeside deck of the hotel, people scan the slopes and lakeshores with binoculars. They search for bears, mountain goats, and bighorn sheep on the mountainsides, and moose, deer, beavers, and bears along the shores of Swiftcurrent Lake.

Many ranger-led activities take place at the hotel in July and August, including hotel tours, guided walks, and evening programs. Check the park newspaper for information.

The hotel opens in June and closes in September. During some winters the winds blow so hard that huge snowdrifts reach the third-story windows of the hotel.

Guess What?

At the Many Glacier Hotel, the bellhops (men who carry luggage to the rooms) still wear Swiss lederhosen (leather shorts with H-shaped suspenders) as their uniform. It's a reminder of the history of the railway and early days of Glacier.

☐ I Saw Many Glacier Hotel!

When?

What was it like?

Glacier National Park has more than 700 miles of hiking trails. If you only have time for a short walk, these are among the best. Along with the beautiful scenery, don't forget to look for animals, plants, colorful sedimentary rocks, and other things described in this book.

☐ I took a hike!

Where?

How far did you hike?

What did you see?

Trail of the Cedars

Distance: *1 mile loop on boardwalk and packed-gravel trail (wheelchair accessible)*
Location: *Avalanche Creek in the McDonald Valley (Shuttle bus stops here)*

Stroll through an ancient forest of western red cedars where some of the mammoth-sized trees are more than 500 years old. This forest is unique in the Rocky Mountains. The trees are similar to the ones found in the temperate rainforests of Oregon and Washington.

About halfway along the trail you'll come to Avalanche Gorge—one of the most photographed places in the park. Notice how the power of water shaped the rocks along the gorge. Look at the colorful rocks in Avalanche Creek.

Hidden Lake Overlook

Distance: *3 miles (round-trip)*
Location: *Logan Pass (Shuttle bus stops here)*

The trail to Hidden Lake Overlook is a steady climb, so take your time. Besides, it's fun to stop and look around. You're in the high country with lots of "big mountain views." This is the land of mountain goats, marmots, and many other critters. Flowers grow everywhere in the meadows and along snowmelt streams. Be sure to stay on the trail so you don't trample plants that are easily damaged. Watch for ripple marks and mud cracks in the large rocks.

Hidden Lake Overlook

Baring Falls

Distance: *1.5 miles (round-trip)*
Location: *Sun Point on the eastern side of Going-to-the-Sun Road (Shuttle bus stops here)*

Baring Falls

The trail starts by Sun Point picnic area. Take the short climb to the top of Sun Point for expansive views of St. Mary Lake and the mountains. Then return to the Baring Falls Trail which winds in and out of the trees and offers additional views of the lake.

The gushing water of Baring Falls comes from Sexton Glacier. While at the falls, check the creek for a small, stout, dark-gray bird. It's called a dipper. If you're lucky enough to see one, it will probably be bobbing up and down (dipping) on a rock. Dippers walk and swim under water in search of aquatic insects. They build their nests behind waterfalls.

Swiftcurrent Lake Nature Trail

Distance: *2.5 miles (round-trip)*
Location: *Swiftcurrent Picnic Area in Many Glacier Valley*

There's lots of evidence of wildlife along this trail. Look for bear claw marks on lodgepole pines and for aspen trees cut down by beavers.

Swiftcurrent Lake

When you reach the boat dock at the head of Swiftcurrent Lake, you've hiked about three-quarters of a mile. At this point you have choices. You can turn around and return to the picnic area where you started (making it about a 1.5 mile round-trip hike) or continue around the lake, past Many Glacier Hotel, and back to the picnic area.

Tips for hiking in Glacier:

★ Check trail information

★ Always hike in groups

★ Go prepared for any kind of weather

★ Bring drinking water and snacks (or lunch and turn it into a picnic hike)

★ Enjoy watching wildlife, but keep your distance (and never feed them)

★ Pack out all your trash

★ Take only pictures (you can't collect anything in the park)

Swiftcurrent Lake trail

I Met a Park Ranger!

There are many kinds of park rangers. The first ones you see might be at the entrance stations where they collect entrance fees and provide park maps. Rangers at the visitor centers provide information, lead walks, and give talks about nature and history. Some rangers work as law enforcement officers. Others hike or ride horses in the backcountry, checking trail conditions or monitoring bear activity.

Rangers will help you learn about Glacier. Stop at any of the visitor centers to pick up a free Junior Ranger activity book. Complete the activities and ask a ranger to check it over. Then you'll be awarded a Glacier National Park Junior Ranger badge.

The Apgar Nature Center is fun to visit. The nature center is located in a small log cabin tucked into the woods by Apgar Village. Here you can see and touch animal furs, antlers, and sedimentary rocks. Throughout the day, rangers give short talks about wildlife, flowers,

A ranger leads a program at the Apgar Amphitheater

Park ranger's hat

Guess What?

Glacier National Park also has scientists, wildlife biologists, trail crews, carpenters, maintenance workers, computer programmers, and many other employees. Together they help keep the park the special place it is and help you enjoy it.

☐ I met a park ranger!

Ranger's Autograph:

Where:

When:

geology, and the people who lived here before Glacier became a park.

Check the park newspaper (handed out at the entrance stations) for all the park's ranger-led activities. These free activities include guided hikes, evening slide shows, and campfire talks. Special programs such as star gazing and Native American dancing, drumming, and storytelling are also offered throughout the summer.

Teepee exhibit at St. Mary Visitor Center

St. Mary Visitor Center

When you see a ranger, say hello. You'll know them by their green and gray uniforms, their badges, and their distinctive "flat" hats. Ask about the kind of work they do and their favorite things about Glacier. Maybe you'd like to become a park ranger or work for the National Park Service. Don't forget to ask a ranger to autograph the opposite page in the box.

More Things I Saw Checklist

Glacier National Park has 71 mammal species, more than 260 bird species, over a thousand plant species, and countless special places including waterfalls, lakes, and mountain peaks. Of course, there's no way to see everything in one trip. But in addition to the items already described in this book, here is a list of other things to watch for. Check off what you see, and good luck!

Mammals
- [ ] Elk
- [ ] Coyote
- [ ] Pika
- [ ] River otter
- [ ] Snowshoe hare
- [ ] Wolf

Grouse

Birds
- [ ] Dipper
- [ ] Harlequin duck
- [ ] Chickadee
- [ ] Clark's nutcracker
- [ ] Black-billed magpie
- [ ] Hummingbird
- [ ] Grouse
- [ ] Ptarmigan
- [ ] Golden eagle
- [ ] Osprey

Pika

Mountains
- [ ] Heaven's Peak
- [ ] Mount Oberlin
- [ ] Clements Mountain
- [ ] Reynolds Peak
- [ ] Garden Wall
- [ ] Going-to-The-Sun Mountain
- [ ] Grinnell Point
- [ ] Mount Sinopah

Dipper

Heaven's Peak

Places
- [ ] Lake McDonald Lodge
- [ ] Sunrift Gorge
- [ ] Sun Point
- [ ] St. Mary Falls
- [ ] Two Medicine Lake
- [ ] Running Eagle Falls
- [ ] Glacier Park Lodge

Other Things I Saw
- [ ] _____
- [ ] _____
- [ ] _____
- [ ] _____

Lake McDonald Lodge

48